The Civil War

Karen Taschek

Copyright © 2009 Bailey Publishing Associates Ltd

Produced for Chelsea House by Bailey Publishing Associates Ltd, 11a Woodlands, Hove BN3 6TJ, England

Project Manager: Patience Coster
Text Designer: Jane Hawkins
Picture Research: Shelley Noronha
Artist: Deirdre Clancy Steer

Library of Congress Cataloging-in-Publication Data
Taschek, Karen, 1956-
  The Civil War / Karen Taschek.
    p. cm. — (Costume source books)
  Includes bibliographical references and index.
  ISBN 978-1-60413-381-3
  1. Clothing and dress—United States—History—19th century—Juvenile literature. 2. United States—Social life and customs—1783–1865—Juvenile literature. I. Title. II. Series.

GT610.T37 2009
391.009034—dc22

                  2008047262

The publishers would like to thank the following for permission to reproduce their pictures: American Civil War Society: 8–9, 30, 31, 33, 41; Bailey Publishing Associates Ltd: *contents page*, 16; Bridgeman Art Library: 5 (Private Collection/Ken Welsh), 6 (© Atwater Kent Museum of Philadelphia/Courtesy of Historical Society of Pennsylvania Collection), 35 (Private Collection/Peter Newark Military Pictures), *imprint* and *contents page detail*, 42 *detail*, 43 (Hirshhorn Museum, Washington D.C., USA), 44 (Private Collection), 46 (© Collection of the New-York Historical Society, USA); Corbis: *title page detail* (© Bettmann), 5 *detail* (© Bettmann), 8 *top* (© Historical Picture Archive), 10 (© Sunset Boulevard/Sygma), 10 *detail* and 13 (© Cynthia Hart Designer), 14 (© Cynthia Hart Designer), 17 (© Bob Krist), 20 *detail* (© Bettmann), 39 (© Richard T. Nowitz), 54 *detail* (© Bettmann), 59 (© Corbis/Sygma); Library of Congress: 21, 24 *detail*, 32 *main*, 32 *detail*, 42; Mary Evans Picture Library: 26, 51; Kobal Collection: 18 (Warner Bros/First National/Hurrell, George), 19 (Selznick/MGM), 50 (Universal/Clifford, John), 52 (Selznick/MGM), 56 (Warner Bros); Military History Division, Smithsonian: 38 *bottom*; Harry T. Peters, "America on Stone" Lithography Collection, National Museum of American History, Behring Center, Smithsonian Institution: 48; Photographic History Collection, National Museum of American History, Smithsonian Institution: 22; Rex Features: *title page*, 15, 20, 25, 23, 34, 40, 45, 49, 53, 58; Topfoto: 6 *detail* (Roger-Viollet), 7, 12, 16 (City of London/HIP), 24 (©Jeff Greenberg/The Image Works), 28 (KPA/HIP), 29, 36 (Jeff Greenberg/The Image Works), 38 *top* (Ann Ronan Picture Library/HIP), 50 *detail*, 54 (The Print Collector/HIP), 55.

Contents

Introduction

The American Civil War (1861–65), also known as the War Between the States, started when eleven Southern states that supported slavery seceded from the United States and formed the Confederate States of America (the Confederacy). Led by Jefferson Davis, they fought against the US federal government (the Union), which was supported by all the free states and the four slave-holding border states.

In some ways, clothes styles during the Civil War changed little, as people waited to see what the outcome of the conflict would be, but some new styles did develop. For example, women officially became nurses for the first time in the North and donned the simple, practical clothes required for their new job. Meanwhile Southern women, short of store-bought materials, returned to sewing clothes as their grandmothers had. On both sides of the conflict, men in uniform became commonplace. These soldiers decorated their basic uniforms with insignia from the many battles.

This book will show you how to dress as people did during the Civil War so that you can perform in plays, parades, and other re-enactments. You can dress up as a Union or Confederate soldier, a nurse, a carpetbagger, or as a slave. Now that we have ready-made fabrics and convenient Web sites, Civil War clothes can be sewn or ordered fairly easily. You may have noticed from the photographs of the time that clothes had a certain look, just as clothes do now. Not everyone dressed the same during the war, but you can often recognize from photographs or paintings the particular Civil War styles. You will want to capture this look when creating the costumes of the period.

Right: The Civil War quickly became a long conflict with ferocious battles between the blue (Union) and the gray (Confederates).

A LONG WAR?

"You people of the South don't know what you are doing. This country will be drenched in blood, and God only knows how it will end . . . Where are your men and appliances of war to contend against them? The North can make a steam engine, locomotive or railway car; hardly a yard of cloth or a pair of shoes can you make . . . Only in your spirit and determination are you prepared for war."

Union general William Tecumseh Sherman, December 1860

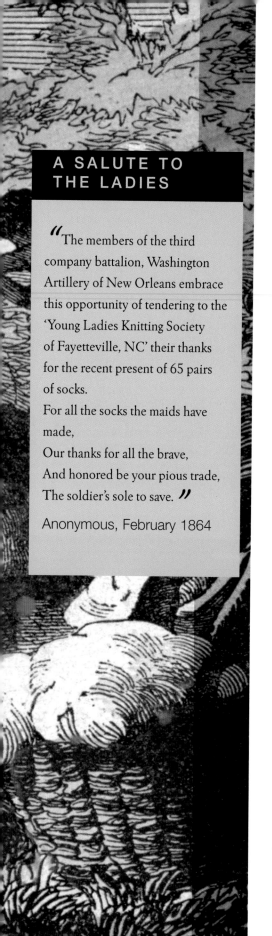

CHAPTER 1

War Begins

"The members of the third company battalion, Washington Artillery of New Orleans embrace this opportunity of tendering to the 'Young Ladies Knitting Society of Fayetteville, NC' their thanks for the recent present of 65 pairs of socks.

For all the socks the maids have made,

Our thanks for all the brave,

And honored be your pious trade,

The soldier's sole to save. "

Anonymous, February 1864

NORTH AND SOUTH

In 1861, most people in the United States didn't think a civil war would really happen. Or if war did come, people of both the North and the South—the two parts of the country—were sure it would be short. Each side was certain it would win. The South consisted of the states of Virginia, North Carolina, Tennessee, Arkansas, Texas, Louisiana, Mississippi, Alabama, Georgia, South Carolina, and Florida. If the South won, slavery would be preserved. The North comprised the states of Maine, Vermont, New Hampshire, Massachusetts, Rhode Island, New Jersey, Connecticut, Pennsylvania, Ohio, Michigan, Indiana, Illinois, Iowa, Kansas, Wisconsin, Minnesota, Oregon, and California. If the North won, slavery would be abolished for good. Slavery was the issue that threatened to tear the United States apart.

Above: The Southern and border states (gray), Union states (pink), and new territories (blue) are shown on this nineteenth-century map. Because the map was made nine years before Oregon joined the Union, this state is shaded blue, not pink.

KING COTTON

In 1861, the country's economy was booming—the North had manufacturing, including textile mills that made cloth, and the South provided cotton to make that cloth. Eli Whitney's invention of the cotton gin in 1793 caused a huge increase in Southern cotton crops. The cotton gin used spikes to separate the seeds from what was called short-staple cotton, which had short fibers compared to long-staple cotton. Short-staple cotton could be grown as far west as Mississippi, not just on the coast. Between 1820 and 1860, cotton production in the South increased sixfold. The South led the world in the production of cotton fiber and shipped millions of bales to textile plants in the northern United States and Britain.

But not all of the people in the South shared in the prosperity. Of the nine million people living in the Southern states, four million were slaves. The South's economy was based on slave labor to pick cotton and tend the other crops. "Cotton is king," announced James Henry Hammond, a Southern planter and politician, adding, "and the African must be a slave."

Tensions in the United States grew over slavery as the country itself grew. New states were asking to be admitted to the Union, and many people didn't want any more states to allow slavery. The Missouri Compromise of 1820 had admitted Missouri as a slave state to the Union, but prohibited slavery in territories north of Missouri's southern border. Then the Kansas-Nebraska Act of 1854 let newly formed

Below: Slaves work a Southern cotton plantation in *The Harvest* (1884), produced by printers Nathaniel Currier and James Ives. The slaves picked and baled the cotton, then drove it to market.

territories decide if they would allow slavery or not, overturning the Missouri Compromise. People in the South felt they had the right to own slaves, just the same as any other property.

PRESIDENT LINCOLN

Abraham Lincoln was elected president of the United States on November 6, 1860. People in the Southern states were convinced that he would abolish slavery, although he didn't say he would right away. Southern states began to secede from the Union. South Carolina was the first to do so, on December 20, 1860, and the other Southern states soon followed. Jefferson Davis was elected president of the Confederacy on February 18, 1861. On April 12, 1861, the Confederates fired shots on Fort Sumter, South Carolina, when the commander of the fort, Major Robert Anderson, refused to surrender it to them. And so the Civil War began.

Above: Abraham Lincoln appears in this photo with his trendsetting lawyer-statesman look in clothing.

STYLE TIP

Before television and radio, people climbed up on a stump or soapbox to get their point across to a crowd. Politicians, in particular, favored this way of drumming up support, and Abraham Lincoln often gave speeches outdoors when he was running for president. For plays and re-enactments, posters advertising a particular point of view can be useful props; for example, placards championing anti-slavery (Northern) or states' rights (Southern) or just saying "Vote for Abe!"

THE FORTUNES OF WAR

The war determined how people dressed during the period, and many people's fortunes changed at that time, especially in the South. A great number of Southerners lost their grand plantations and the ownership of the slaves who had picked cotton from the land and made the plantation owners rich. Southerners in the path of Union general William Tecumseh Sherman lost everything as the general and his men marched through Georgia in late 1864, burning and looting in a 300-mile swath. Most Northerners, who were on the winning side, did better after the war ended. Some Northerners moved to the South right after the war to take advantage of opportunities there. Southerners called these newcomers carpetbaggers and disliked them intensely.

Below: A present-day Civil War re-enactment at Gettysburg uses very realistic costumes and includes a Confederate flag.

FABRICS

Fabrics used to make clothes in Civil War times were cotton, linen, wool, and silk. Most fabric was manufactured, not woven at home, and people could buy many different weights and weaves of fabric even outside the city. Fabric came in every possible color and shade. People's choice of material and how much they used showed how wealthy they were. Fine clothes were made from silk (the most expensive material), chintz (a fine cotton cloth), and good-quality wools rather than plain cottons. Cloth isn't manufactured in exactly the same way now and cannot be matched perfectly when one makes a Civil War costume. But some fabrics are very authentic—the polished cotton of today looks much like silk, for example, and is close enough for a Civil War look.

CHAPTER 2

Antebellum and Civil War Dress: Women

WHAT WEALTHY WOMEN WORE

Fashions for wealthy women at the start of the Civil War were based on French, English, and Northern styles. Charles Frederick Worth, who had clothing boutiques in England and France, was the main influence on antebellum (the time before the Civil War) fashions. Wealthy Southern families vacationed in the North to escape the hot summers and while they were there bought American versions of the latest European fashions. The richest plantation families traveled to Europe so that the women could buy a new wardrobe in Paris and the men could buy the latest styles in London. Seamstresses came to the homes of these families to make their everyday clothes.

CLOTHES FOR A BALL

At the start of the Civil War, a woman going to a ball might choose a gown made of a material such as silk tulle in a soft color, for example peach or pink. (Modern substitutes for silk tulle are rayon or nylon tulle.) The ball gown typically had a dropped neckline to reveal the shoulders

Above: Scarlett O'Hara (Vivien Leigh) in the 1939 movie *Gone With the Wind*, is the all-time icon of a wealthy, plantation-owning Southern woman.

APPROPRIATE ATTIRE

In the movie *Gone With the Wind*, Vivien Leigh plays Scarlett O'Hara, the "belle of six counties" in Civil War Georgia. Early on in the movie, Scarlett insists on wearing a very low-cut dress to a barbeque at the neighboring Wilkes family home. However, Mammy, one of the O'Hara house slaves, tells Scarlett, "You kain show yo' buzzum befo' three o'clock," reflecting the attitudes of contemporary nineteenth-century society—that it was improper for a woman to show too much flesh during the daytime.

Hair parted in the middle and flat, looped back over ears

A Civil War-era Southern belle in a ball gown

Dropped, off-the-shoulder neckline

Fitted bodice shows off tiny waist

Rose pattern of gown is repeated in bracelet, at bosom, on sleeves, and in hair

Bracelet

Overskirt with hooped skirt beneath

Small print, silk fabric

The four flounces on the overskirt make it circular

and a banded skirt with the bands trimmed in lace. By the nineteenth century, lace and net trim were machine made and affordable, so a ball gown could be decorated lavishly with them. Flowers, such as camellias or roses, were often worn in the hair, with a cluster of the same flower at the bosom. Matching slippers completed the outfit.

DRESSING FOR THE DAY

When today's woman gets dressed in the morning, she might put on underwear, jeans, a shirt, socks, and shoes and be good to go most places in a few minutes. Before the Civil War, dressing was a time-consuming activity. Women had to don many complicated layers of clothes before they could go out for the day or even work around the house.

First they put on their underwear, a shift or chemise made of cotton or linen over a pair of long-legged drawers made of the same material. The underwear was often decorated with lace or ribbon. Next came the corset, which was stiffened with whalebone stays and laced down the back. Corsets made a woman's waist look small compared to her shoulders, sleeves, and hips, which was the look she wanted. Since women hoped to end up with the tiniest waist possible (a fifteen-inch waistline was ideal),

Below: Women show off their drawers in the 1954 movie *Seven Brides for Seven Brothers*, about seven unruly men in 1850s Oregon who must be tamed to attract wives.

Above: Godey's Lady Book shows women's fashions at the beach around the time of the Civil War. Clearly the covered-up look was in vogue.

the stays often had to be laced extremely tight. A corset also helped a woman be the same size every day so that she could fit into her tightly molded bodice.

The morning's dress ensemble was completed with the crinoline, or hoop skirt, which gave the skirts of antebellum women their classic bell shape. In the 1850s, women wore several petticoats to puff out their skirts, including a wool one in the winter and an outer petticoat that was tucked and embroidered. By the late 1850s, the petticoats had been replaced by the crinoline, a frame of steel hoops. Hoop skirts had steel supports and could be as much as six feet across, although they were usually only four feet across. During the war, the pleats of skirts were at the front, whereas postwar skirts were flat at the front. As the war continued and the price of the cheapest calico material rose to $25 per yard, Southern women could no longer afford enough material to cover the wide hoops and didn't wear them.

As women moved around the house, which would have been filled with lighted candles and lamps, they had to be careful that their enormous skirts did not catch on fire. The cage of the hoop skirt was

THE FASHIONABLE WOMAN'S BIBLE

Godey's Lady Book was an expensive fashion magazine launched in Philadelphia in 1830 by Louis A. Godey and Charles Alexander. *Godey's* wasn't just a fashion magazine—it included poetry, short stories, and even sheet music. Women in the North and South read the fashion pages of *Godey's* to see the latest styles worn in Paris, shown on hand-tinted color plates. The magazine included tips for accessorizing and choosing the proper wear for an event, together with dress patterns and advice on choice of fabrics and colors. *Godey's* began to lose readers to competing magazines, such as *Ladies' Home Journal* and *Harper's Bazaar*, in the 1880s and finally stopped publication in 1898.

WEDDING DRESSES

Although white was often worn, many women married in one of their better dresses of any color. A bride might spend more money on a fine quality of fabric than on fancy trim. Weddings were usually held during the day, so wedding dresses were day dresses, with jewel (plain, slightly rounded) necklines and long sleeves. Wedding attendants often dressed just like the bride instead of in differently styled bridesmaid dresses. Marriages could be large and formal, if the couple had money, or simply consist of a private visit to a local clergyman.

often covered with the fabric crinoline, which is where the skirt got its name. To finish dressing, a woman put on her bodice, skirt, and shoes. Before the war, bodices extended below the natural waist. After the war, the bodice was above it. Shoes were either high topped, resembling granny boots, or slippers, worn for balls.

GOING OUT

Antebellum women wore capes, cloaks, and shawls to keep out the cold. In very cold weather, a woman could wear the lovely pelisse-mantle: a long cloak lined or trimmed with fur or made out of fur. A matching fur hat and muff completed the look. Capes draped over the dress and didn't usually cover it all. They were often made of solid fabrics, but a different fabric from the dress. Shawls, in paisley, large check, and many other patterns, were popular. A light-colored lace shawl was worn with a dark dress and a dark lace shawl with a light or a dark dress. Fancy cloaks

Below: Godey's shows women's and children's wedding fashions.

were bought as one-of-a-kind and even had names—for example, a cloak called the Alma came from G. Brodie's, a shop on Canal Street in New York City.

When they went out, women wore bonnets, tying them with ribbons under the chin. Bonnets could be re-trimmed to meet the latest fashion. During the war, the brims of bonnets became taller and the sides were cut back until the bonnets were spoon shaped. Most women did not wear caps, indoors or out, although movies often portray them this way. Older women might wear simple, usually white or light-colored caps that completely covered their hair and tied under the chin. Younger women, when they wore a cap at all, wore one that covered only the back of the head. These caps were often dark colored and trimmed with lace.

Above: Nicole Kidman as Ada in *Cold Mountain* (2003) wears an elaborate beribboned hat and is much more neatly dressed than Jude Law (on the left), who plays Inman, Ada's beloved in this Civil War story.

SLEEPWEAR AND LEISUREWEAR

Women wore long nightgowns to bed, which might have puffy sleeves with lace inserts. Around the house, women wore dressing gowns. The dressing gowns were often made of thin silk in the summer and of satin or brocade (heavier silk) in the winter. The woman put the dressing gown on over her underclothes and hoop skirt and might wear a cap of matching material.

CLOTHES FOR HOUSEWORK

A woman's work dress to do chores around the house might be made out of the material gingham, with the bodice lined with canvas for warmth. A woman could take off her hoop skirt to do work in the garden or heavy

chores in the house. Both men and women wore an apron for work, whether in the house, a butcher shop, or elsewhere. Work aprons weren't usually white but were made of fabrics with small prints to hide stains. Aprons followed the lines of dresses, full at the hips and hem.

ACCESSORIZING

Jewelry was indispensable to accessorize an outfit, but the pieces were smaller during the Civil War than later in the nineteenth century. Rose gold was the preferred kind of gold for jewelry, but all golds were more common than silver. Human hair was woven and arranged into two- and three-dimensional patterns and worn in earrings, brooches, and bracelets. Earrings dangled from long French wires. Brooches were shaped in horizontal or vertical ovals. Large, bold bracelets were a popular item, sometimes worn in matched pairs, one on each arm. Belts weren't worn before the Civil War, but later, jewelry and belts were worn at the waist to emphasize it. Belts were made of fabric and fastened with hooks and eyes—any buckles were just for decoration.

Right: Fans and nosegays, fashionable handheld accessories of the time, are featured in *Godey's*.

Left: A Scarlett O'Hara look-alike appears a bit out of place against the skyline of modern-day Atlanta, Georgia, one of the character's haunts in *Gone With the Wind*.

STYLE TIP

To appear a fine young lady, it might be necessary to order a hoop skirt from a Web site. An old prom dress from an older sister might, with a little adjustment, make an excellent Southern belle ball gown. Someone's wedding gown is another possibility, but it will need to be returned to the owner in good shape. Silk, the material used to make fancy ball gowns during the Civil War, is still expensive today, but nylon makes a good substitute. And remember, no wristwatches, please! Women wore watches on chains that could be tucked into a belt or pocket at the waist, and men had pockets in vests for their watches. Eyeglasses can be worn as long as they're small and have octagonal or oval frames and wire rims.

When gloves were worn, they went only to the wrist to make the hands look fashionably plump. At the time of the Civil War, gloves were manufactured and sold in many kinds of leather and colors: yellow, blue, green, pink, and gray.

Because skirts had to lie smoothly over hoops, they couldn't have pockets, so women carried purses. Some women carried a reticule, a small drawstring bag, or a "long purse"—a long cylinder of net or crocheted work closed at the end. The purses were quite small.

Fans were popular accessories. In the 1860s, they were small, 6 to 10 inches (15 to 25 centimeters) when closed. Fans came in many varieties: a round, homemade fan could be made of palmetto (leaves from a kind of palm tree), or the fan could be a traditional shape, covered with paper or silk and sometimes painted. Women often carried handkerchiefs, usually made of fine lawn or muslin (cotton fabrics woven of extremely fine threads). Nicer handkerchiefs were trimmed with embroidery, forming initials, bees, butterflies, and many other patterns.

A parasol made of fine silk or lace added an elegant touch. A nosegay, or a small bunch of flowers in the hand, made women smell nicer—this was before indoor plumbing made bathing easier and deodorant was invented. During Civil War times, washing daily became a fad (and one that stuck), so each bedroom had a pitcher and basin.

Right: Bette Davis as Julie Marsden in the movie *Jezebel* (1938) is a coquette much like Scarlett O'Hara in *Gone With the Wind*. Like Scarlett, she eventually sees the heartlessness of her ways and tries to reconcile with her man. Note her accessories, which include gloves and a reticule, and her hair, elaborately ringleted for a special occasion.

HAIR AND MAKEUP

Hairstyle was very important in antebellum times since it contributed to the look women wanted of a round, full face. To that end, women parted their hair down the middle, then pulled strands down over the cheeks and looped them back up over the ears into a knot or bun. For an ordinary day, a woman would smooth her hair back into a bun. Hair was styled flat on top. Evening hairstyles included more curls and tendrils. As the war dragged on, women began to skip time-consuming hairstyles. Women in the Civil War period are often portrayed in movies wearing hairnets, also called snoods, but photographs rarely show this. If a hairnet was worn, it was almost always dark, made of fine thread in a fishnet pattern.

Most antebellum women didn't wear makeup since it was associated with "ladies of the evening"—women who spent time in bars and other

disreputable and unhealthy places and needed makeup to touch up their color. Sometimes respectable women would wear rouge or powder, but pale skin and lips were signs that a woman was at leisure and didn't have to work all day in the sun.

WHAT POORER WOMEN WORE

A woman wearing a silk gown and lace accessories clearly did not belong to the same class as a woman in a dress made of coarse fabric, wearing an apron. Poorer women needed to wear their clothes as long as possible. They fashioned them from fabrics such as osnaburg (a coarse inexpensive linen), fustian (a cotton and linen mix), linsey-woolsey (a blend of linen and flax), or other poor-quality wools. They bought fabric with small prints so that if they cut material from the dress to repair it or make it more fashionable, the print would match more closely. Panels of dresses made with solid fabrics could be turned inside out when the material became worn or faded. Fabric collars attached to a dress could be removed when worn or soiled.

THE PROTEST THAT BACKFIRED

Amelia Jenks Bloomer was an early American feminist who wanted to reduce the enormous size of the hoop skirt, which she saw as a form of bondage for women. Bloomer expressed her views on the subject in her temperance magazine, *The Lily.* She invented the Bloomer dress in 1850, with a tight bodice, short skirt, and baggy pants gathered at the ankle. But her effort backfired when women put the Bloomer top over a skirt with yet another flounce, reaching to the floor.

CHAPTER 3

Antebellum and Civil War Dress: Men and Children

Antebellum men didn't wear any item of clothing that was as distinctive as the hoop skirt. However, a man who belonged to the upper class, in his tailored shirt, stylish coat, and velvet breeches, could easily be distinguished from a working man, in his loose shirt (so that his arms were free for physical work), short jacket, and pants or leather or osnaburg breeches.

Businessmen of all kinds adopted the distinguished look of statesmen. Abraham Lincoln personified this dignified look of the lawyer-statesman.

Right: Clark Gable as Rhett Butler in *Gone With the Wind* dresses in well-cut clothes made of good materials as befit a wealthy gentleman.

Men wore a sober black suit, white linen, a tall silk hat, a black or red cravat (scarf tie), and boots or gaiters (leg coverings that went from the ankle to the midcalf or knee).

Above: This group includes government employees and soldiers, giving a good representation of the clothing of the time.

The tall, straight-sided hat that Lincoln usually wore was called a stovepipe. (Sometimes Lincoln stored documents under his roomy hat.) English bowler hats, known as derby hats in North America, became fashionable during the war. They were made of felt with a low, dome-shaped crown and narrow brim.

For underwear, men often wore union suits (so named not because these men showed loyalty to the Union but because the undergarment was one piece). Loose pants were fashionable for men during the Civil War, and a generally rumpled look was in style. Suspenders were often worn instead of belts. A man's day wear might consist of a frock coat of black or brown wool, matching pants, and a brocaded satin vest or waistcoat. The cravat could be starched to stand out, and a top hat and boots, the commonest footwear of the time, would complete the outfit. In winter, wool clothes were worn for warmth. When the war began, many men wore their uniforms as day wear and also to formal occasions, such as balls. Men at this time wore their hair parted in the center, and had long sideburns and often mustaches and beards.

The many photographs from Civil War times show how people dressed. Photography was new then, and people loved to get their photograph taken. But do the images show how people really dressed, or were they in their "Sunday best"? Probably most of them were in their regular, or typical, clothes. In those days, people didn't have drawers stacked with T-shirts—only the wealthiest people would have had many outfits. Material was expensive, and rather than buy or make new clothes, people often redid outfits. Most of the soldiers who posed for photographs during the Civil War were dressed in their regular uniforms, since few could have afforded a special uniform for picture taking.

During the Civil War, it became fashionable for girls to wear a uniform inspired by European military heroes. This consisted of a skirt, a bolero jacket with wide bell sleeves, and a garibaldi blouse. This was a loose, often red blouse that was fuller at the bottom than the top and had trim on the cuffs and front. It was named after the Italian patriot Garibaldi, who visited England in 1863.

A working man might be found in a blue denim pullover shirt (buttons all the way down a shirt weren't worn at the time) and cotton pants, with suspenders or a sash instead of a belt. A felt hat with a medium-size crown and brim completed the outfit.

CHILDREN'S CLOTHES

Boy and girl babies wore long gowns with wide necklines and short sleeves. These garments were longer than the babies themselves so that they would stay covered and warm in their cribs. The gowns were

Below: This photo shows a typical Civil War family, with the children already wearing clothes similar to the adults'.

shortened as children grew older so that they could walk. Boys and girls were both dressed in gowns and skirts so that diapers could be easily changed. Children wore their hair in a blunt cut to below the ears.

Girls' dresses often had wide, low-cut, boat necklines and short sleeves. The dresses were about knee length and showed pantalets underneath, often edged with lace. Later in the war, skirts covered the pantalets. A fancy dress might be made of velvet or silk, trimmed with lace and paired with white shoes, stockings, and spats. Teenage girls lengthened their dresses from midcalf to ankle, then to the floor, and grew their hair longer than they had as young children.

As boys grew up, they began to wear vests and hats, and they got their first pair of boots when their feet stopped growing, probably at about age twelve. A boy dressed up for an evening out might wear a suit of black broadcloth trimmed with black satin ribbon at the cuffs and the bottom of his frock coat. Under his knee-length pants would be black stockings with black shoes and spats. A derby hat with a feather in the hatband provided the finishing touch.

Above: Shirley Temple stars in the movie *The Littlest Rebel* (1935) with John Boles as her father, Confederate captain Herbert Cary. Southern girl Virgie Cary (Temple) cares for her ailing mother while her father is at war, and even charms President Abraham Lincoln.

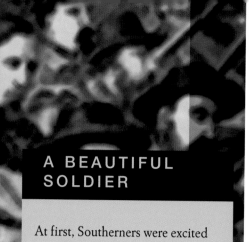

CHAPTER 4

Southern Uniforms

At first, the South seemed to be gaining in the Civil War. It won two big battles in Virginia—the First Battle of Bull Run on July 21, 1861, and the Battle of Fredericksburg, from December 11 through 15, 1862. For a while, the clothes of Southern people reflected their success—they went on with their old ways from before the war, when Southerners had plantations, money, and slaves and attended extravagant balls in elegant dress.

A BEAUTIFUL SOLDIER

At first, Southerners were excited and optimistic about the war. Mary Chesnut, an aristocratic resident of Charleston, South Carolina, wrote in her diary around the time of the Confederate attack on Fort Sumter:

"Preston Hampton is in all the flush of his youth and beauty, six feet in stature; and after all only in his teens; he appeared in fine clothes and lemon-colored kid gloves to grace the scene."

Above: The Confederate soldiers in this re-enactment scene wear an assortment of headgear, including slouch hats and forage caps (kepis).

Soon, though, war shortages caught up with everyone. Fashion stood still in the South for most of the Civil War years, as women altered and mended old clothes. Southern women of all social classes found themselves wearing sunbonnets and simple dresses to do field work and raise crops to feed the army. Finally, even the beautiful ball gowns had to be ripped into pieces to provide bandages for the wounded. The best costume that most women could achieve was an ordinary muslin dress with gourd-seed buttons. Southern women had always made most of their children's clothes, as well as underwear for their families, and work clothes for the men. Now they turned to making uniforms for the soldiers.

THE BLUE AND THE GRAY

The official colors of soldiers' uniforms in the Civil War came to be blue for the North (the Union) and gray for the South (the Confederacy). But in 1861, at the start of the war, Confederate uniforms were a hodgepodge of colors and styles. The Confederacy was a new country, and, unlike the Union, it had no army in place. So the first volunteers in the Confederate army set off for war wearing whatever they had, either their regular clothes, an old uniform from an earlier war, or a uniform sewn by the women at home. Before the war, both the North and the South had militias, small groups of part-time soldiers. The uniforms for the militias were sometimes blue in the South, gray in the North, or green on either side.

Once the battles began, the different colors of uniform caused confusion. At the First Battle of Bull Run, regiments from Virginia in the South were wearing blue uniforms when they charged Union batteries (groupings of big guns). The Union soldiers did not recognize them as enemies until it was too late. In 1862, Jefferson Davis, the Confederate president, established cadet gray as the official color for Confederate uniforms, but the dye needed to achieve that color was in short supply. The uniforms turned out many shades of gray, a shade of brown called

Above: In *Gods and Generals* (2003), a movie with painstakingly accurate historical costumes, Robert Duvall stars as General Robert E. Lee (in the pale hat). Civil War battles are also carefully re-created in the movie.

Left: In this painting, General Stonewall Jackson is shown wearing the uniform of a Confederate officer, with the extra touch of a plumed hat.

"butternut," and, sometimes, light blue. Even soldiers in the same regiment weren't dressed alike. To make matters worse, the uniforms became worn quickly, making them even harder to distinguish from Northern uniforms.

Soon after the war began, the Confederate government issued its first "Great Appeal" for clothing for the soldiers. Wives, daughters, and sweethearts of soldiers formed volunteer aid societies to sew new gray uniforms and socks for the soldiers to wear through the winter of 1861. The second Great Appeal for soldiers' clothes was issued in fall 1862 and helped to clothe the Confederate soldiers until the end of 1864, after the fall of the Southern cities Atlanta and Vicksburg. Near the end of the war, Confederate soldiers wore whatever they could find, including captured Union uniforms.

A CONFEDERATE ARMY DISGUISED

The famous Confederate general Thomas J. "Stonewall" Jackson led his troops in the First Battle of Bull Run on July 21, 1861, wearing the uniform of a colonel of the Union Army. Behind him, the uniforms of his troops from the 4th and 27th Virginia regiments looked almost like the uniforms of the Yankees across the battlefield.

THE EVOLUTION OF CONFEDERATE UNIFORMS

At first, the variety in Confederate uniforms was endless since all the uniforms came from home. During the winter of 1861–2, the Confederate Quartermaster Department in Richmond, Virginia, provided some uniforms for the soldiers, but not enough, and many soldiers were left wearing rags and had no shoes. As a result, each Southern state began to produce its own uniforms, funded by a government system begun in July 1861 giving each soldier $21 (about $450 in today's dollars) every six months for uniforms. The C. S. Army Regulations issued in 1861 stipulated how uniforms were to look and that they be made of gray cloth.

Confederate uniforms changed quite a bit during the war. Despite the regulations, the soldiers from one Confederate state never looked much like the soldiers from any others. Although the uniforms were all gray in accordance with the regulations, the shades of gray were very different because of dye shortages and variations. To re-create this look for your own Confederate regiment, use different colors of gray for coats and pants and vary the style of hats between slouch hats and kepis.

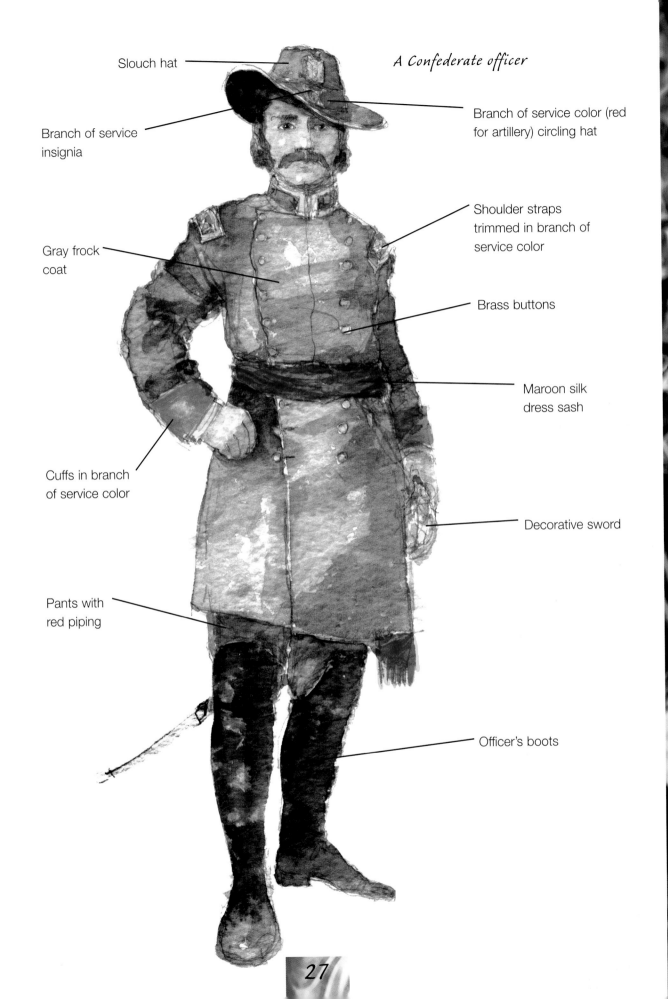

Slouch hat

Branch of service insignia

Gray frock coat

Cuffs in branch of service color

Pants with red piping

A Confederate officer

Branch of service color (red for artillery) circling hat

Shoulder straps trimmed in branch of service color

Brass buttons

Maroon silk dress sash

Decorative sword

Officer's boots

Right: Generals Robert E. Lee (Martin Sheen) and James Kemper (Royce D. Applegate) discuss Confederate strategy in this scene from the movie *Gettysburg* (1993). General Kemper is quite the swashbuckler here with his long white gloves and sword. General Lee was always impeccably dressed.

THE CONFEDERATE IRISH

Of the 109 men in Company I, 8th Alabama, 104 had been born in Ireland. Their uniforms were dark green. Their flag had a Confederate battle flag on one side with George Washington in the center. On the other side it was green, with a harp, shamrocks, and the slogans *Erin go bragh* ("Ireland forever") and *Faugh a ballagh* ("Clear the way").

WHAT CONFEDERATE OFFICERS WORE

Confederate army regulations specified at the beginning of the war that Confederate officers wear a coat based on an Austrian design. But by 1862, a year into the war, the long gray frock coat worn by General Robert E. Lee had become commonplace. The coats, made by the officers' tailors, could be single or double breasted and might show the colors for the branch of service, such as red for artillery or yellow for cavalry, on the cuffs or collar. Short shell coats became popular later in the war because they used less material. The coats could be made of many materials, including English broadcloth, wool and cotton blends, or homespun wool. A buff or maroon silk sash was worn by all officers.

Confederate army regulations directed officers to wear a forage cap, but many wore the comfortable slouch hat. Since the officers bought their own hats, they designed many varieties. The slouch hat might have gold or black cords around the top of the hat and insignia showing the officer's branch of service. Confederate officers also helped themselves to Union slouch hats after a battle. Officers often bought their own boots.

WHAT CONFEDERATE ENLISTED MEN WORE

Enlisted men usually wore the short shell jacket. The jackets were made of various kinds of gray or butternut wool and cotton, including twill, jean cloth, and kersey. Jacket sleeves might be trimmed with colored tape to show branch of service or because a soldier liked that color. Pants were made of wool or cotton homespun.

Rather than wear the regulation forage cap, soldiers often chose slouch hats or palmetto straw hats. The forage caps, usually gray or butternut in color, were made of cotton or wool jean cloth with brims of leather or oilcloth. Slouch hats were usually black or brown, with a

Below: In this re-enactment, Confederate soldiers in a variety of uniforms have formed a firing line for a mock battle.

star or state insignia attached. Enlisted men often acquired Union brogans and boots as footwear. For a time, the Confederate Quartermaster Department manufactured the same style of brogans as the Union ones.

BELTS, BUTTONS, AND RANK INSIGNIA

Belts were usually black or dark brown and fastened by belt plates. The plates could be many shapes, such as rectangular and oval, with different insignia on the front. A common insignia was *C. S.* or *C. S. A.*, for *Confederate States* or *Confederate States of America*, but states also produced their own belt plates, such as a lone star for Texas.

Uniform buttons, usually made of brass, might be from state militias the soldiers had belonged to before the war or were United States rather than Confederate Army issue. On the front of the buttons sometimes a letter indicated the branch of service (such as *A* for artillery), or the buttons might be inscribed with an eagle or a state seal. On collars, the number of stripes and stars on a strip of gilt lace indicated rank; for example, a second lieutenant wore one stripe, a first lieutenant two stripes, a major one star, and a colonel two stars. All general officers (officers above the rank of colonel) wore showy gilt cord galloons (trim with scalloped edges) on their coat sleeves. As the war went on, some officers left off the galloons to avoid attracting snipers.

EQUIPMENT

Confederate soldiers carried the C. S. Richmond rifled musket, a gun made at the Richmond Armory and Arsenal; it was accurate up to 600 yards. Soldiers also carried canteens, usually made of wood or metal (don't spoil the Civil War look by carrying a canteen made of plastic or another modern material). Sometimes they packed a knife to skin rabbits or scale fish. The soldiers put what personal items they had into haversacks, which looked like big leather purses and hung from a shoulder strap. A soldier might put rations, eating utensils, a tobacco pouch, a Bible, and photographs of loved ones into the haversack.

Often Confederate soldiers had to do without tents and sleep on blankets on the ground. They rolled all their possessions into the blanket and slung it over their

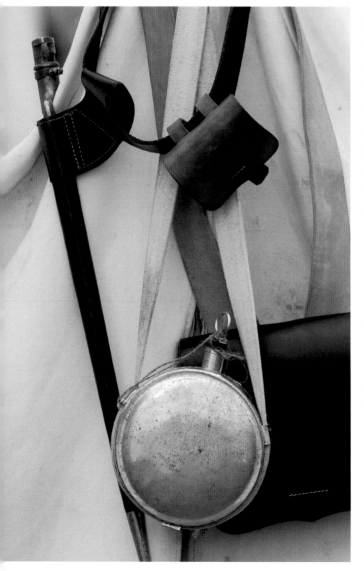

Below: Confederate soldiers carried wood or tin canteens, but few wood ones survived. Some canteens had *C.S.*, for *Confederate States*, on the side.

shoulder, tying it at the waist. In this way they could travel light over the many miles they marched to battle.

BATTLE FLAGS

At the beginning of the war, battle flags for the North and South looked similar, as did uniforms. Neither side worried much about this at first, since both were convinced that the war wouldn't last long and that victory would be theirs. But as the summer of 1861 wore on, Northerners and Southerners realized the war wouldn't be over soon. Each side needed a distinctive battle flag because the soldiers couldn't tell the flags apart. This contributed to deaths from "friendly fire" since the soldiers couldn't tell friend from foe and killed men on their own side. In November 1861, near Centreville, Virginia, the first Confederate battle flag was given to Confederate officers. The flags varied in color from light pink to red, since scarlet silk couldn't always be found. Silk didn't wear well, so the next batch of flags was made of scarlet bunting. Special flags were sometimes made by the women at home.

Below: A drum corps was an important part of keeping soldiers in step on a march and boosting morale. Sometimes the drummers were young boys, as in this re-enactment scene.

WEAPONRY

The Confederacy acquired weapons when soldiers captured arsenals that had belonged to the United States but were now in Confederate territory. Since the South had no manufacturing facilities for weapons at the start of the war, soldiers set off with their fathers' or grandfathers' swords and guns from past wars. The swords were of little use against the new quick-loading guns, and the new guns outmatched the old ones. As the war went on, the Confederacy was able to buy guns from England and other countries. Confederate soldiers also took weapons from Union soldiers killed in battle.

Northern Uniforms

At the beginning of the war, textile manufacturers cut corners to meet the sudden demand for uniforms, using compressed fibers of recycled wool goods to make a material called "shoddy." This word entered the language as a description of poor workmanship. General Ulysses S. Grant said of his soldiers' uniforms: "The clothing received has been almost universally of an inferior quality and deficient in quantity."

Above: Union soldiers from the 7th New York State Militia relax in front of their tent, posing for their portrait. In between battles, soldiers kept busy by mending clothes, cleaning equipment, playing cards, and writing home.

At first, the Union suffered terrible losses in the Civil War. The worst were at Antietam, on September 16, 1862; in Sharpsburg, Maryland, on September 17, 1862; and at Fredericksburg, Virginia, on December 13, 1862. At Antietam, 12,401 Union soldiers and 10,316 Confederate soldiers were killed, wounded, or listed as missing in just one day. At Fredericksburg, the casualties were 12,653 for the Union and 5,377 for the Confederates. After the loss at Fredericksburg, President Abraham Lincoln said, "If there is a worse place than Hell, I am in it." But the situation could have been worse for the North. Until the Battle of Gettysburg, the Civil War was fought almost solely in the South. Supplies to the North, including cloth and other manufactured goods, were not disrupted nearly as much as in the South, so both soldiers and civilians were better clothed.

UNIFORM SHORTAGE

In 1860, the North manufactured 94 percent of the cloth and 90 percent of the boots and shoes in the United States. But at the beginning of the war, as in the South, soldiers' uniforms for the army were in short supply.

In early 1861, the US Quartermaster, who was in charge of clothing the army, supplied the regular US Army of 16,000, but President Lincoln called for 75,000 troops to volunteer for the war. The task of clothing all those additional soldiers was assigned through contracts to seamstresses and tailors. The quality of uniforms supplied to the soldiers by US manufacturers was poor until the government threatened to buy its cloth in England instead.

Until the production lines got up to speed, Union soldiers fought in all kinds of uniforms. The 3rd New York regiment, the 1st Vermont regiment, and almost all the soldiers from Indiana wore gray uniforms with black trim, just like the Confederate soldiers from Georgia. The 1st

Above: In this re-enactment, the curled horns on some of the men's hats indicate infantry. The US flag and a regimental flag are an essential part of the group.

Iowa regiment wore uniforms like those of soldiers from Louisiana, and the soldiers from Maine, Kansas, and Nebraska all wore gray. Even in 1862, the second year of the war, recent recruits at the Battle of Shiloh in Tennessee fought in all different kinds of uniform and regular clothes.

WHAT UNION OFFICERS WORE

To avoid mix-ups on the battlefield, US Army regulations decreed that blue pants and blue tops be standard for its uniforms. Officers usually wore long frock coats, double breasted for higher-ranking officers and single breasted for lower ranking. Sack and shell coats were also allowed.

Officers' pants were made from a loose-weave wool or the heavy jeanlike material, linsey-woolsey, and were fastened with metal buttons (no zippers), which were also used as suspender buttons. They had no back pockets, only side pockets, and no belt loops. The pants weren't ironed or creased. They had a one-eighth-inch strip in the outside seam of the legs, colored to show branch of service, for example, red for artillery.

Officers often wore forage caps or, especially in the West, slouch hats. General Ulysses S. Grant, commander of all Union forces at the end of the war, was always to be seen in a slouch hat. The forage cap was made of blue wool, whereas the slouch hat was made of brown or black felt. On the front of forage caps was the men's branch of service plate, such as

Below: Both Major Dundee (Charlton Heston) and his horse appear to be yelling in this scene from the movie *Major Dundee* (1965). The Union major wears blue pants with a yellow strip, indicating the cavalry branch of service.

Left: Ulysses S. Grant, commander in chief of the Union forces, is represented after the Union victory at the Battle of Chattanooga, Tennessee (November 23–25, 1863). Grant, who was notoriously careless about his appearance, looks unusually neat in this painting.

BLACK HATS AT GETTYSBURG

On July 1, 1863, several groups of soldiers clashed at the Battle of Gettysburg, including the Union's Iron Brigade. The Iron Brigade faced the troops of Confederate A. P. Hill, who was joined by Major General Richard Ewell's 2nd Corps. The Iron Brigade was formerly known as the Black Hat Brigade because of the tall felt black hats the men wore. The hats had on the front a red cloth circle, along with the brass numerals and letters required by the army to indicate what unit they belonged to.

crossed cannons for artillery or a curled horn for infantry. The branch of service plate was gold thread embroidered on black velvet. A cord around the hat brim was the color of the branch of service.

WHAT ENLISTED MEN WORE

Enlisted men usually wore sack coats made of dark blue flannel that fit loosely (which is why they were called "sack" coats). They had four buttons and were single breasted. Name tags, such as a starred badge pinned to the coat with the soldier's name on it, could be used to identify him if he was killed.

The pants of enlisted men were made of sky blue kersey. Like the officers' pants, they had side pockets, no belt loops, and closed with buttons. Leg strips showed the branch of service. Enlisted men's shirts were usually made of coarse wool, sometimes flannel, and were white, gray, or dark blue. Two to four buttons, usually bone, fastened the shirts, which were pulled over the head. The shirts had no pockets.

At first, enlisted men wore a piece of colored cloth on top of their forage caps to show officers what division they belonged to. Later the insignia was made of stamped brass and worn on the front of the hat. Different designs, such as circles and stars, were assigned to corps, and different colors were assigned to divisions within the corps: red was the first division, blue was the second division, and white the third. Soldiers proudly put the insignia on their canteens and haversacks as well. The forage caps also had plates of service like those of the officers.

The Union issued its soldiers with shoes called Pattern 1851 Jefferson brogans. These ankle-high boots came in different sizes, and soldiers were required to blacken them. (Bootblack could be gotten from the sutler, a civilian who provisioned the army.)

Below: Soldiers appear to be fixing bayonets in this re-enactment. Few bayonet charges actually occurred during the Civil War since the soldiers hated that bloody, close-contact fighting.

Wool forage
cap, or kepi

Shoulder strap in
branch of service
color (red for artillery)

Haversack

Single-breasted
frock coat with a
single row of buttons

Pants made of
linsey-woolsey

Red strip
for artillery

Enlisted man's
boots

A Union officer

Branch of service
insignia

Brass buttons

1861 Springfield
rifled musket

Pattern 1851 sword
belt with brass plate

During the war, some soldiers wore unusual hats. Zouaves could be soldiers fighting for either the Union or Confederacy, since the Zouave uniform was actually French and copied by both sides in the Civil War. Zouaves modeled their uniforms on the Zouaves of the French Army, who had won a reputation as daredevils in the Crimean War (1854–6). The Zouave battle cry was, "Zou! Zou! Zou!"

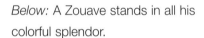

Below: A Zouave stands in all his colorful splendor.

Above: Major General Philip Sheridan was General Grant's right-hand man during the Civil War. Sheridan's cavalry chased down the forces of General Robert E. Lee and helped bring about his surrender in 1865.

BELTS, BUTTONS, AND RANK INSIGNIA

Officers wore a sword belt issued by the army, with a rectangular brass belt plate. Enlisted men wore a regulation black belt with the initials US on an oval brass belt plate. Buttons were made of thin rolled sheet brass. As with Confederate uniforms, Union officers' buttons were usually decorated with eagles, state seals, and a letter identifying the branch of service: the letter *A* for an artillery officer or *C* for a cavalry officer, for example. The number and arrangement of buttons on the frock coat indicated the officer's rank. Buttons arranged in two rows of nine and in groups of three meant the officer was a major general or above; General William Tecumseh Sherman's coat had this arrangement. A brigadier general had two rows of eight buttons, arranged in groups of two.

Shoulder straps on the coat showed an officer's rank. The straps, one on each shoulder, were a patch of velvet the color of the branch of service and bordered with gilt. Rank was indicated by insignia such as stars and bars—for example, one star was a brigadier general, two a major general, and three a lieutenant general. Dress epaulettes, large gilt thread shoulder boards with gilt fringe and with rank insignia on the board, were worn for formal occasions such as parades. The rank of enlisted men was indicated by inverted V chevrons in the branch of service color on the sleeve.

EQUIPMENT

The regulation firearm of the Union infantry was the 1861 Springfield rifled musket, and it was used in every major battle. Union soldiers, like Confederates, also sometimes brought along personal knives. Union soldiers traveled light, sometimes throwing away heavy items such as bayonets, whereas the Confederate soldiers hardly ever had them in the first place. Union soldiers carried haversacks or knapsacks, which they filled with much the same items as Confederate soldiers, although the

Below: A Union soldier aims at an unseen enemy in this re-enactment. Like most Civil War soldiers, he takes his personal possessions, such as his bedroll, into battle for safekeeping.

SAVED SPECIAL FOR SUNDAY

"'Dey was dressed in deir best Sunday go-to-meetin' clothes and deir shoes, all shined up, was tied together and hung over deir shoulders to keep 'em from gittin' dust on 'em.' The men wore 'plain homespun shirts and jeans pants,' and although some of the women wore homespun dresses, 'most of 'em had a calico dress what was saved special for Sunday meetin' wear.'"

Julia Larken, a slave on a plantation in Georgia, remembered years later how the slaves looked as they headed off for church on Sunday; quoted by Frederick Law Olmsted in *Cotton Kingdom*

CHAPTER 6
Slaves' Clothes

THE PECULIAR INSTITUTION

White Southerners called slavery their "peculiar institution," but they were determined to preserve it at all costs. While slavery was the main cause of the Civil War, many white Northerners fought only to preserve the Union and had little sympathy for slaves. Some Southerners also didn't think slavery was right, but almost the entire Southern economy was based on slaves to harvest cotton, sugar, and tobacco.

Cotton production was backbreaking, time-consuming work. First, shovels were used to break up the soil in the fields. Then a harrow, a tool with metal teeth, was used to remove debris and smooth and level the soil. In an old cotton field, the dead stalks from last year's crop had to be

Above: Slave families never knew how long they would remain together—at any time, one or more family members could be sold to a new owner.

beaten down with clubs or pulled out by hand. Then the field was fertilized and planted, also by hand. While the cotton plants grew, they needed thinning out, and the field was hoed for weeds. Then the cotton bolls were picked and ginned (at this point, at last, a machine was involved). Finally the cotton was loaded onto wagons to be taken to market.

Above: Slaves were auctioned off to the highest bidder like any other property.

From the start, slavery was an inhumane practice. Slaves arrived in the United States having endured a six- to twelve-week journey from Africa, jam-packed into the bottom of ships. Many died as a result of the terrible treatment they suffered on the journey. The ones who survived were bought and sold: a healthy black man sold for about $3,000 (more than $70,000 in today's dollars) and a child for $250 (more than $5,000 today). In 1807, importing slaves to the United States was banned, so Southerners used the slaves they had and then used their children. At the time of the Civil War, Southerners wanted to extend slavery into the new western territories of the United States, but many Northerners objected to this plan.

Slaves had nowhere to run away to. The Fugitive Slave Act of 1850 said that even if they escaped to the North, their Southern masters could reclaim them. In 1857, the decision of the US Supreme Court to return former slave Dred Scott to slavery following his master's death in the North further reduced slaves' chances for freedom. Sometimes slaves tried to escape anyway. The Underground Railroad was a series of safehouses set up along routes to the North. Sympathetic people would house and feed the runaways for a time, then pass them along to the next house until the slaves reached the North and relative safety.

In the middle of the Civil War, President Lincoln moved to free the slaves. On September 22, 1862, he announced the Emancipation Proclamation, to take effect on January 1, 1863. Although Lincoln wanted to free the slaves throughout his presidency, he first had to please voters in the border states of Kentucky, Missouri, Maryland, and Delaware and those in the North who believed that the Civil War was being fought to save the Union, not free the slaves. Emancipating the slaves almost cost Lincoln re-election as president in 1864. He said, "If I could save the Union without freeing any slave I would do it, and if I could save it by freeing all the slaves I would do it, and if I could save it by freeing some and leaving others alone, I would also do that."

Below: Slaves who were field hands did backbreaking work from dawn till dusk.

A PAINFUL SHIRT

Slaves' clothes were made of tough materials, such as flax, so that they would last. Booker T. Washington, a famous author and ex-slave, wrote in his book *Up from Slavery* that "the most trying ordeal" he had to endure as a slave was "the wearing of a flax shirt." He compared it to having "a hundred small pinpoints, in contact with his flesh." His older brother, John, once wore a flax shirt of young Booker's for several days until it was broken in, which Booker described as "one of the most generous acts that I ever heard of one slave relative doing for another."

THE SLAVES' CLOTHING

The 400,000 or so slaves who arrived in the United States between 1619 and 1808 brought their own traditions of clothes. Some slaves began to wear the styles of their masters right away. Often they had no choice—the slaves arrived wearing only scraps of clothes, and their masters gave them their own cast-off garments to wear. The new slaves found wearing the heavy, bulky clothes of their masters difficult. They could adjust the clothes to fit, and some masters encouraged their slaves to dress well as a reflection of themselves and their households. Slaves could be divided into house slaves and field hands: those who waited on the master and his family in the house and those who worked the fields.

Difference in tyles of clothes in the United States were not quite as rigid as in Europe, but it was still possible to tell those people who worked with their hands at menial labor apart from those who did not. The clothes of the American wealthy were stylish, fit well, and were clean, whereas slaves' clothes were often just the opposite. To keep slaves in the lowest class of society, South Carolina passed a law in 1735 specifying that slave clothes could only be made of the cheapest fabrics.

Below: In *Gone With the Wind*, Hattie McDaniel played Mammy, a house slave. Mammy was able to dress relatively well and didn't have to work in the fields, a point she makes to Scarlett after the war.

Right: This boy and girl pose in their Sunday best. Since the photograph was taken in 1863, after Lincoln's Emancipation Proclamation, technically the children weren't slaves, although they lived in Louisiana, in the South.

DIARY OF A SLAVE

A famous ex-slave, Frederick Douglass, wore many different kinds of clothes throughout his life. Born into slavery, Douglass wrote in his autobiography that he received the yearly clothing allowance of "two coarse linen shirts, one pair of linen trousers, like the shirts, one jacket, one pair of trousers for the winter, made of coarse . . . cloth, one pair of stockings, and one pair of shoes." He tried to escape to the North several times and at last succeeded, disguised as a sailor. There Douglass was able to live free as a statesman and speaker, wearing fashionable clothes to suit his profession.

But slave owners sometimes used clothes, either hand-me-downs or new clothes, to reward slaves and create a hierarchy, or ranking, among them. Favorites, carriage drivers, house slaves, and especially good field workers might be given better clothes.

After a day of hard work, slave women made their families' clothes at night, in the dim light of the slave cabins. Men made shoes out of cowhide, with wood soles. The shoes were stiff and uncomfortable. Slave children, both boys and girls, dressed in long shirts or smocks until they were at least twelve. Then boys would wear a shirt and pants and girls a dress.

DYEING AND PATCHING

Slaves still developed their own styles of clothes. Runaway-slave posters printed in the North and South show escaped slaves wearing many styles of dress. The slaves spun their own cloth out of cotton they had picked,

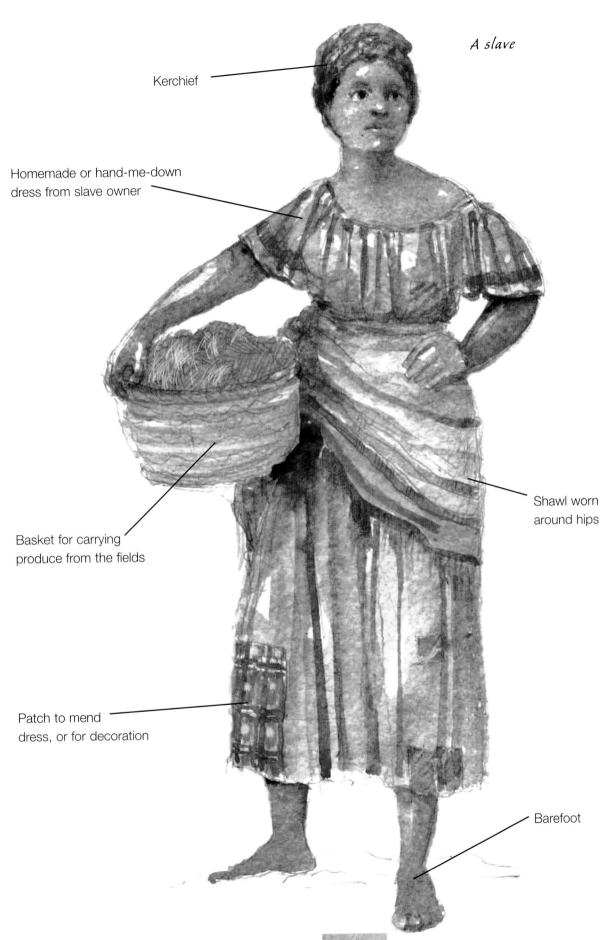

A slave

Kerchief

Homemade or hand-me-down
dress from slave owner

Basket for carrying
produce from the fields

Patch to mend
dress, or for decoration

Shawl worn
around hips

Barefoot

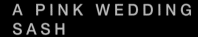
then used dyes and different combinations of colors to create their own styles. Because clothes often had to be patched, slaves would add patches from other garments to create a quilt look, sometimes using bold or clashing colors. The slaves may have brought some of their ideas for the arrangements of colors and patterns from Africa.

Sometimes slaves were allowed to earn money from small garden plots, cutting wood, or other work. They could use the money to buy clothes, and most slaves managed to own special Sunday outfits. Some people thought the slaves in their Sunday best were better dressed than the slave owners.

WEDDING FINERY

Like everyone else in the United States, women slaves tried to look their best for their wedding day. Sometimes all they could do was to clean their existing clothes or get a new set of their everyday wear. Some slaves simply jumped across a broomstick to marry, but most were married by a preacher in a ceremony and in clothes similar to their owners'. Women slaves usually wore white and as fancy a dress as possible, sometimes even borrowing a dress from an owner. Because slaves could be sold and separated at any moment, wedding ceremonies included the vow "Till death or distance do us part."

Below: After the 54th regiment, many regiments of black men, always led by a white officer, were formed. The Confederacy didn't enlist black soldiers because they didn't want to arm former slaves. In this recruitment poster, black soldiers are shown in stylish, well-made uniforms, although this was seldom the case in reality.

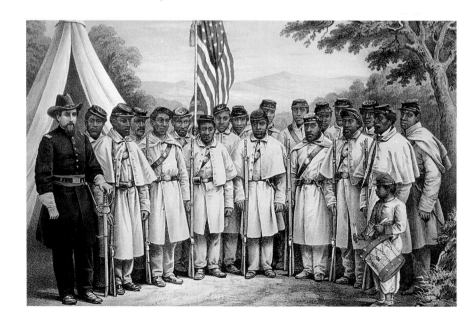

Frederick Law Olmsted traveled throughout the South during the Civil War as a reporter for the newspaper that became the *New York Times*. He commented on slavery in general and the differences between the clothes of the slaves and white people. He noticed that in Richmond, Virginia, the capital of the Confederacy, on Sunday many slaves were "dressed with foppish extravagance, and many in the latest style of fashion." On the better streets "there were many more well-dressed and highly dressed colored people than white; and among this dark gentry the finest French cloths, embroidered waistcoats, patent-leather shoes, resplendent brooches, silk hat, kid glove, and eau de mille fleurs, were quite common."

AFRICAN AMERICAN SOLDIERS

After Lincoln's Emancipation Proclamation freed the slaves, ex-slaves could enlist in the Union Army. The Confederate Army, as much as it needed men, refused to arm slaves to fight. The Union Army paid black soldiers less than white soldiers, usually only assigned them to menial tasks, such as digging ditches, and gave them the poorest-quality clothes to wear.

The 54th Massachusetts regiment, led by Colonel Robert Shaw, was the first black regiment to serve in the Civil War. At first, the men did not have Union infantry uniforms. They were issued uniforms before they left Massachusetts for battle and had the honor of parading through Boston before Governor Andrew and Frederick Douglass. The black soldiers were exceptionally brave, because any black man wearing a Union uniform and captured by the Confederates would be hanged on the spot.

Below: In this scene from the movie *Glory* (1998), Colonel Robert Shaw, played by Matthew Broderick, watches Private Trip (Denzel Washington) of the 54th Massachusetts regiment at target practice.

CLOTHES TO MOURN THE DEAD

As casualties mounted, men and women began dyeing clothes black to show they were in mourning for a husband, brother, son, or friend. Soldiers wore black armbands. Women in heavy mourning wore black clothes, jewelry, veils, and bonnets and covered outerwear with black crepe. Sometimes heavy mourning for a husband lasted more than two years. In the later stages of mourning, women began to wear lighter-colored clothes, such as lavender and gray. A woman might resume social roles and use white handkerchiefs with black borders. Children in mourning wore white with black trim. The custom of a riderless horse at the funeral began in the 1600s or before and was often used in the Civil War, including at the funeral of President Lincoln.

CHAPTER 7

The Blockade of the South

A SHORTAGE OF SUPPLIES

After the loss of Fort Sumter started the Civil War, President Lincoln imposed a naval blockade on the Confederacy on April 19, 1861. The blockade meant that Confederate ships had a very hard time maneuvering around Union warships to bring manufactured goods to the South. It lasted the entire war, during which time the South tried to break through, even sending the ironclad ship the *Virginia* on March 9, 1862, to smash through the blockade near Hampton Roads, Virginia. But the Union sent its own ironclad ship, the *Merrimack*, to face the *Virginia*, and although both ships were damaged, the blockade held.

Very soon, the South ran short of cannons and other weapons to use in the war. Also, because almost all the textile mills for making clothes were in the North or in England, the blockade of the South came to mean shortages of food, clothes, and medical supplies needed by civilians and soldiers. Blockade runners took cotton to Britain and other foreign countries and brought back medicine, rifles, and other wartime necessities, making a huge profit when they got through, but the runners could not bring in enough manufactured goods to supply the South at war.

Below: The movie *Ride With the Devil* examines the disorganized, vicious North-South conflict in Kansas and Missouri.

The Confederate Ordnance Department increased production of arms and ammunition in the South, but for the entire war, clothes and shoes were in very short supply. A Confederate soldier earned only $16 (about $300) a month, but the price of clothes quickly skyrocketed until a pair of boots cost $250 (about $5,000) and a good coat $350 (about $7,000). A pound of butter cost $15 (about $300) and a barrel of flour $1,000 (about $21,000)!

After the blockade took effect, new clothes were almost out of the question for Southerners. Southern women responded to the clothes shortages by taking looms out of attics and weaving homespun cloth, the way their grandmothers had before the days of manufactured cloth. Before the war, the profession of dressmaker hadn't been considered respectable for a woman. People didn't approve of a woman having a job unless it was typical women's work as a governess, a teacher, or a servant.

Now most women found themselves making all the clothes for their families. All women had experience of sewing, but they were also expected to know how to crochet and knit to fill spare moments with useful employment. Sewing circles of women sat in their parlors and spun cloth for uniforms, socks, and other garments for the soldiers. With her circle of acquaintances, Mary Chesnut, a lady of Charleston, South Carolina, knitted socks for General Stonewall Jackson's entire brigade.

Since Southern women couldn't get new clothes during the war, they transferred accessories from one outfit to another to create new-looking styles and wore twice- and thrice-turned dresses. ("Turning" was a polite

Above: As women in sewing circles anxiously awaited word of the war, they stitched clothes for the soldiers.

way of saying they mended old dresses.) Women also made clothes out of rags and curtains, and shoes from carpets and canvas sails. Boots were woven from fronds of palmetto. Sewing needles were hard to come by, so pins were made out of carefully cut thorns. Dried persimmon seeds replaced scarce buttons. To add color to cloth, women used onion skins to make a burnt orange dye and carrot tops to make a greenish yellow dye.

THE BREAD RIOT

Finally, after nearly two years of almost total blockade by the North, Southern women were tired of food and clothing shortages. In Richmond, Virginia, on April 2, 1863, about a thousand women and boys, led by a woman named Mary Jackson, gathered in Capitol Square and walked to the retail district of Richmond. The women and boys would have been in noticeably mended, faded, or poorly dyed clothes in antebellum or early war styles.

Below: A lukewarm supporter of the Southern cause, Scarlett is happy to wear the new bonnet her friend Rhett Butler has run through the blockade.

SCARLETT O'HARA BREAKS THE BLOCKADE

"Wrapped in layers of tissue was a bonnet, a creation that made her cry: 'Oh, the darling thing!' as she reached for it. Starved for the sight, much less the touch, of new clothes, it seemed the loveliest bonnet she had ever seen. It was of dark-green taffeta, lined with water silk of a pale-jade color. The ribbons that tied under the chin were as wide as her hand and they, too, were pale green. And, curled about the brim of this confection was the perkiest of green ostrich plumes. "

Margaret Mitchell, *Gone With the Wind*, 1936

Left: In the movie *Cold Mountain*, Renée Zellweger plays Ruby, a friend of Ada (Nicole Kidman). The two women farm in Civil War Cold Mountain, North Carolina. Here Zellweger is dressed in a simple work outfit of the time.

A SADLY MOLTING CONDITION

"A party had come to Columbia who said they had run the blockade—came in by flag of truce &c. Colonel Goodwyn asked me to look around and see if I could pick out the suspected crew. It was easily done. We were all in a sadly molting condition. We had come to the end of our good clothes in three years, and now our only resource was to turn them upside down or inside out—mending, darning, patching. . . . The handsomest of the three women had a hard Northern face. All in splendid array—feathers, flowers, lace, jewelry. "

Mary Chesnut, *Civil War*

As the women walked to town, they broke windows and looted the stores of speculators (the hated people who acquired scarce goods, then sold them at high prices). The women and boys gathered armloads of food and clothes and piled them in wagons. By the time the crowd reached Main Street, shopkeepers had heard they were coming and closed up. The mob smashed windows and doors, then helped themselves to more food and clothes and also jewelry and silks. A group of soldiers marching in stopped the looting. Then Richmond's mayor read the Riot Act to the mob, threatening to order the soldiers to shoot people if they didn't disperse.

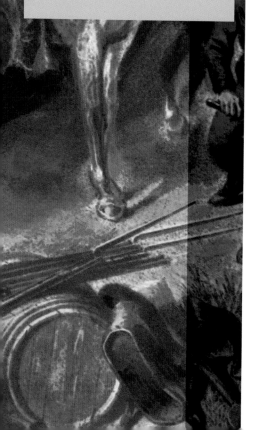

CHAPTER 8

The North's Victory and Reconstruction

OUR BELOVED CONFEDERACY

"Dear M., in her sadness, has put some Confederate money, and postage stamps into a Confederate envelope, sealed it up, and endorsed it, 'In memory of our beloved Confederacy.' I feel like doing the same, and treasuring up the buttons, and the stars, and the dear gray coats, faded and worn as they are, with soiled and tattered banner, the untarnished sword and other arms, though defeated, still crowned with glory."

Judith McGuire, journal

THE BITTER END

After the North won the Battle of Gettysburg (July 1–3, 1863) in Pennsylvania, fought by the armies of Generals Robert E. Lee and George Meade, the South never stood a chance of winning the Civil War. General Lee surrendered the Army of Northern Virginia to General Grant at Appomattox Court House, Virginia, on April 9, 1865,

Below: The Union win of the Siege of Vicksburg cut the Confederacy's supply lines, including the imports of goods and weapons through Mexico that had avoided the Union blockade.

finally ending the war. The Civil War had not been short at all. It had lasted almost four full years, from the firing of the shots on Fort Sumter on April 12, 1861, to Lee's surrender at Appomattox. It had been a terrible slaughter— more than 600,000 soldiers had died from battle injuries or disease.

Unfortunately for the South, President Lincoln was assassinated at Ford's Theater in Washington on April 14, 1865. Vice president Andrew Johnson succeeded Lincoln as president on April 15, 1865. The Reconstruction of the South turned out to be quite different from what Lincoln had planned, "with charity toward all and malice toward none."

TROUBLED TIMES IN THE SOUTH

After the Confederate surrender, Union soldiers gathered in Washington for a huge victory parade in their honor. Southern soldiers walked or rode home, however they could, to start over in the ruined South. They were hungry and dressed in rags, what was left of their Confederate uniforms or Union uniforms taken after battles. At home, the women, children, and old people who awaited them were also badly off. Four years of war and blockades had reduced food and clothing to the barest of minimums.

Northerners flocked to the destroyed South, hoping to make money. Sometimes they carried large cloth suitcases, or carpetbags, in which they could stuff loot from abandoned Southern homes. "Carpetbagger" was the name given by Southerners to anyone from the North living in and making money from the South. In the South, many of the fields of plantations had been burned and the buildings bombed, and the slaves were now free and didn't have to help repair them. Formerly wealthy Southerners had to sell the plantations, work the plantations themselves, or find something else to do.

The typical costume of a carpetbagger is shown in a scene from the movie *Gone With the Wind*. Scarlett O'Hara tries to keep Tara, the family plantation, going with the help of her family and a few ex-slaves. Wearing a big quilted sunbonnet and a neat but simple red print dress with puffed sleeves and no hoop skirt, Scarlett picks cotton under the hot

Above: Some Confederate soldiers began the war in fine uniforms, but by the end of the war, almost all were dressed in whatever clothes they could get. Even the always impeccably dressed General Lee was wearing his last good uniform when he surrendered to General Grant at Appomattox.

Right: With the addition of a hat, gun belt, and boots, Josey Wales (Clint Eastwood) is transformed from a farmer into an outlaw in the movie *The Outlaw Josey Wales* (1976), about life in the post-Civil War West.

sun, the top buttons of her bodice undone. Scarlett's shoes are badly torn. Gerald O'Hara, Scarlett's father, who has lost his mind from grief after his wife's death, is wearing a ruffled dress shirt, open at the neck, and a rumpled, double-breasted coat of an expensive material such as velvet.

A carpetbagger, Jonas Wilkerson, drives by a line of ragged, bandaged Confederate soldiers walking home. In Wilkerson's comfortably upholstered open carriage is a conspicuous, multicolored carpetbag with leather handles. The carpetbagger wears a brown derby, a red cravat, a double-breasted brown frock coat, a white shirt, and suede gloves. Riding with him, taking his ease and singing, is a black man in a green vest, a black derby, a silk lavender cravat, a dark green double-breasted coat, and leather boots. He carries a cane with a large gold handle.

Derby

Bootlace tie

Striped shirt

Fancy embroidered vest

Velvet frock coat

Carpetbag with
leather handles

Contrasting lining

Checked, unmatching
pants

Well-made new boots

NEW STYLES FOR A NEW LIFE

After the Civil War ended in April 1865, people in the North and South picked up the pieces of their lives as best they could and tried to go back to normality. Women's fashions quickly changed, still guided by the fashion magazines *Godey's Lady Book* and *Harper's Bazaar*. The large skirt of the mid-1860s became a smaller skirt in the late 1860s, looped up in the back and called a polonaise skirt, a style inspired by eighteenth-century fashion. Waistlines moved up a bit from the natural waist. Women's dresses often had Watteau back pleats, also revived from the eighteenth century and named after the artist Antoine Watteau, who painted subjects in dresses with these box pleats on either side of the dress's back center. The pompadour (rectangular) neckline and the Marie Antoinette fichu, an often frilly scarf draped over the shoulders, were other eighteenth-century revivals.

Right: The TV show *The Big Valley* starred Barbara Stanwyck as a strong-willed mother homesteading with her four sons in California after the Civil War. The rectangular neckline of Stanwyck's dress, together with its rich fabric and bright color, reflect the changing styles in women's clothing in 1870s America.

Left: Actor Tommy Lee Jones played an Old West cowboy in *Lonesome Dove* and *The Missing*. Many ex-Confederates, such as the outlaw Jesse James, went West after the Civil War in search of a new life.

CIVIL WAR COSTUMES

Re-enactment enthusiasts who don't want to buy a ready-made costume can with a little time and effort make one out of ordinary clothes. Thrift stores are good sources of inexpensive clothes that can be modified into Civil War costumes; for example, a gray or blue wool suit coat with the collar turned up is half of a Union or Confederate uniform. Yellow fabric can be purchased cheaply to make collars, designs, and sashes for the uniforms. Sew brass buttons to the coat, adding gold star buttons for the collar. Gold or yellow yarn can be used to make epaulettes for the coat's shoulders, attached with hot glue. Felt can turn a baseball hat into a Union hat. Looking at a picture of a uniform helps in the design, and you can be as accurate as you want. Alternatively, many Web sites sell inexpensive Civil War costumes for children and adults.

Instead of long, heavy cloaks, women substituted paletots, which had a top and partial overskirt. *Harper's Bazaar* advised making paletots in such colors and fabrics that they could be worn with different skirts. After the drab war years, women favored sumptuous fabrics and bright colors.

During Reconstruction times, more men, especially in the South, were businessmen and professionals, not plantation owners, and they dressed in much the same styles as during the war. Unlike President Lincoln, President Andrew Johnson, whose clothing style included high collars and huge neckties, was not much imitated.

Many former Confederate soldiers, who had lost all they owned in the war, drifted West to start a new life as cowboys. Cowboys' clothes were always functional: they wore high boots and pants of a thick material such as denim to avoid sores from all day in the saddle, a loose shirt, and a hat with a broad brim to keep the sun and rain off the face.

Eventually, the South recovered economically. But the plantation life, with its glamorous costumes for the wealthy, never returned.

Glossary

antebellum Before the American Civil War.

arsenal A place where arms or military equipment are made or stored.

artillery Large-bore mounted firearms, manned by more than one person, such as cannons.

blockade runner A person or ship that avoided the Union naval blockade of the Southern coasts.

bolero jacket A loose jacket that is open at the front.

border states Kentucky, Missouri, Maryland, and Delaware. These states were slave states but stayed in the Union during the Civil War.

brocade Silk with raised patterns in gold and silver.

chemise A woman's one-piece undergarment, often made of cotton.

chevron Two diagonal stripes that meet at an angle, usually with the point up.

Confederacy The states that seceded from the Union in the Civil War. Those states were Virginia, North Carolina, Tennessee, Arkansas, Texas, Louisiana, Mississippi, Alabama, Georgia, South Carolina, and Florida.

Confederate A person who fought for the South in the Civil War or believed in the South's cause.

cravat A band or scarf worn around the neck.

crinoline A skirt made of steel hoops held together by muslin bands and with a waistband.

derby A stiff felt hat with a dome-shaped crown and narrow brim.

enlisted man A man in the armed forces ranking below the officers.

fichu A woman's scarf worn draped over the shoulders and fastened in front.

forage cap (kepi) A hat with a short visor, or brim, and round flat top worn by officers and enlisted men of the North and South.

frock coat A man's knee-length coat, usually double breasted.

gaiters A cloth or leather leg covering worn by men that reached from the ankle to the midcalf or knee.

galloon A narrow trimming with both edges scalloped.

gingham A plain woven cotton fabric in stripes, checks, plaid, or solid colors.

haversack A bag with a strap worn over the shoulder.

housewife A sewing kit containing needles and thread as well as toiletries and other personal items.

infantry Foot soldiers led by officers.

insignia Distinguishing emblems on soldiers' uniforms, caps, or weapons.

kersey A heavy wool or wool and cotton fabric.

osnaburg A coarse, plain inexpensive type of linen.

paisley A fabric, usually soft wool, woven or printed with colorful, curved, abstract figures.

paletot A substitute for a cloak that only partially covered the skirt.

quartermaster An officer in charge of procurement and supply of clothing, tents, and other supplies.

sack coat A long military jacket with a straight back.

secede To withdraw from an organization.

shell jacket A short military jacket.

slouch hat A broad-brimmed hat often worn by officers in the Civil War in place of the forage cap.

spats Cloth or leather gaiters covering the instep and ankle.

speculator In the Civil War, people who acquired scarce goods and sold them at high prices.

tulle A sheer, often stiffened silk, rayon, or nylon net often used for veils or ballet costumes.

Union The states left after the secession of the Southern states. Those states were Maine, Vermont, New Hampshire, Massachusetts, Rhode Island, New Jersey, Connecticut, Pennsylvania, Ohio, Michigan, Indiana, Illinois, Iowa, Wisconsin, Minnesota, Oregon, Kansas, and California.

Further Information

BOOKS

Chesnut, Mary. *Mary Chesnut's Civil War*. Yale University Press, 1981.

Crane, Stephen. *The Red Badge of Courage*. Signet Classic, 2004 [1895].

Davis, Burke. *The Civil War: Strange and Fascinating Facts*. Wing Books, 1960.

Leisch, Juanita. *An Introduction to Civil War Civilians*. Thomas Publications, 1994.

Leisch, Juanita. *Who Wore What? Women's Wear, 1861–1865*. Thomas Publications, 1995.

Mitchell, Margaret. *Gone With the Wind*. Scribner, 1936.

Olmsted, Frederick Law. *The Cotton Kingdom: A Traveller's Observations on Cotton and Slavery in the American Slave States, 1853–1861*. Da Capo Press, 1996 [1861].

Smith, W. C. III. *Reenacting the War Between the States*. Lyons Press, 2002.

Stowe, Harriet Beecher. *Uncle Tom's Cabin*. Chelsea House, 2008 [1852].

Troiani, Don. *Regiments & Uniforms of the Civil War*. Stackpole Books, 2002.

WEB SITES

www.buycostumes.com
Buy a General Robert E. Lee costume, including uniform, hat, sash, and sword, or an Abraham Lincoln costume with stovepipe hat, vest, pants, and even a beard.

www.clicket.com
Outfit kids and adults for your Civil War re-enactment, play, or trick-or-treat group. Kids can get a Scarlett O'Hara *Gone With the Wind* red Southern belle costume. You can assemble armies from both sides of the conflict and outfit a child or adult Abraham Lincoln as well. This Web site provides a good selection of gowns for both women and girls attending your ball, but the men will have to wear their uniforms—no fine linen suits are sold here.

www.homeschoolinthewoods.com
A homeschool teacher explains where to find the basics and how to put them together to make the outfits of a Union soldier, a Confederate soldier, or a Clara Barton. The materials are inexpensive and the costumes a bit time-consuming but easy to make.

www.ushist.com
This Web site supplies would-be Confederates and Unionists who plan to be the next John Wayne or Denzel Washington. It's for the adults in your group, both in the sizes of the costumes and the prices. If you order from this site, you can get every detail right, from the insignia on your cap to a hospital tent.

www.shootingstarhistory.com
Here you can buy patterns for everything, from men's Civil War-era shirts to parasols from the Shooting Star Enterprises Web site. The site also gives suggestions for materials that can substitute for Civil War-era ones.

www.suvcw.org/reenact.htm
A Web site listing dozens of re-enactment societies, including the Civil War Skirmish Association and the American Civil War Re-enacting Society, many of them specializing in certain regiments. The societies can answer questions about the uniforms of those regiments.

Source List

A selection of movies, TV series, and musicals with Civil War themes.

MOVIES

Abraham Lincoln (1930), dir. D. W. Griffith, with Walter Huston, Una Merkel

Andersonville (1996), dir. John Frankenheimer, with Jarrod Emick and Frederic Forrest

The Birth of a Nation (1915), dir. D. W. Griffith, with Lillian Gish, Henry B. Walthall

Cold Mountain (2003), dir. Anthony Minghella, with Jude Law, Nicole Kidman

The Coward (1915), dir. Thomas H. Ince, Reginald Barker, with Frank Keenan, Charles Ray

The Drummer of the 8th (1913) dir. Thomas H. Ince, with Cyril Gardner, Frank Borzage

Drums in the Deep South (1951), dir. William Cameron Menzies, with James Craig, Barbara Payton

The General (1927), dir. Clyde Bruckman, Buster Keaton, with Buster Keaton, Marion Mack

Gettysburg (1993), dir. Ronald F. Maxwell, with Tom Berenger, Martin Sheen

Glory (1998), dir. Edward Zwick, with Matthew Broderick, Denzel Washington

Gods and Generals (2003), dir, Ronald F. Maxwell, with Jeff Daniels, Robert Duvall

Gone With the Wind (1939), dir. Victor Fleming, George Cukor, Sam Wood, with Vivien Leigh, Clark Gable

The Good, the Bad, and the Ugly (1967), dir. Sergio Leone, with Clint Eastwood, Eli Wallach

Granddad (1913), dir. Thomas H. Ince, with William Desmond Taylor, Mildred Harris

The Great Locomotive Chase (1956), dir. Francis D. Lyon, with Fess Parker, Jeffrey Hunter

The Horse Soldiers (1959), dir. John Ford, with John Wayne, William Holden

How the West Was Won (1962), dir. Henry Hathaway, John Ford, George Marshall, with Debbie Reynolds, Henry Fonda

The Little Foxes (1941), dir. William Wyler, with Bette Davis, Herbert Marshall

The Littlest Rebel (1935), dir. David Butler, with Shirley Temple, John Boles

Major Dundee (1965), dir. Sam Peckinpah, with Charlton Heston, Richard Harris

An Occurrence at Owl Creek Bridge (*La Rivière du Hibou*) (1962), dir. Robert Enrico, with Anne Cornaly, Roger Jacquet

The Outlaw Josey Wales (1976), dir. Clint Eastwood, with Clint Eastwood, Chief Dan George

The Proud and the Damned (1972), dir. Ferde Grofé Jr., with Chuck Connors, Peter Ford

The Red Badge of Courage (1951), dir. John Huston, with Audie Murphy, Bill Mauldin

Ride with the Devil (1999), dir. Ang Lee, with Tobey Maguire, Jonathan Rhys Meyers

Shenandoah (1965), dir. Andrew V. McLaglen, with James Stewart, Doug McClure

Wicked Spring (2002), dir. Kevin Hershberger, with Brian Merrick, D. J. Perry

TV

The Blue and the Gray (1982), dir. Andrew V. McLaglen, with Gregory Peck, Sterling Hayden

The Colt (2005), dir. Yelena Lanskaya, with Ryan Merriman, Steve Bacic

Gettysburg: Three Days of Destiny (2003), dir. Robert Child, with Steve Schlosser, Bob Bosler

North and South (1986), dir. Richard T. Heffron, with Patrick Swayze, Kirstie Alley

Secret Soldiers of the Civil War (2006), dir. Robert M. Wise, with Madaline LaRocque, Shannon Knopke

The Shadow Riders (1982), Andrew V. McLaglen, with Tom Selleck, Sam Elliott

DOCUMENTARIES

Aftershock: Beyond the Civil War (2006), dir. David Padrusch

The Civil War (1990), mini-series, dir. Ken Burns

Civil War Battlefields: Gettysburg/Wilderness/ Spotsylvania/Appomattox (2007), Timeless Media Group

Civil War Combat: America's Bloodiest Battles (1999), dir. David de Vries, Jim Lindsay

Civil War Combat: The Battle of Franklin (2002), dir. Robert M. Wise

Civil War Combat: The Battle of Fredericksburg (2003), dir. Robert M. Wise

Civil War Combat: The Bloody Lane at Antietam (2000), dir. David de Vries

Civil War Combat: Little Round Top at Gettysburg (2002), dir. Robert M. Wise

Civil War Journal: Vol. 1, *John Brown's War*; Vol. 2, *Destiny at Fort Sumter*; Vol. 3, *The Battle of 1st Bull Run*; Vol. 4, *The 54th Massachusetts* (1993), dir. Donna E. Lusitana

Civil War Life: Left for Dead (2002), dir. Mark Bussler

Civil War Life: Shot to Pieces (2002), dir. Mark Bussler

Civil War Minutes: Confederate (2001), dir. Mark Bussler

Civil War Minutes: Union (2001), dir. Mark Bussler

Civil War Terror (2007), History Channel

The Last Days of the Civil War (2003), History Channel

Reconstruction: The Second Civil War (2005), PBS

*Roots of Resistance: The Story of the Underground Railroad (*1989), dir. Orlando Bagwell

Secret Missions of the Civil War (2005), dir. Darryl Rehr

Sherman's March (2007), dir. Rick King

Women and the Civil War (2005), dir. Ed Dubrowski

MUSICALS

The Civil War (1999), song cycle by Frank Wildhorn, Gregory Boyd, and Jack Murphy

Rebel Cry (2003), lyrics by Linda Nell Cooper, music by David Legg

Reunion (1999), play by Jack Kyrieleison and Ron Holgate, music arranged by Michael O'Flaherty

Shenandoah Christmas (2000), lyrics by Linda Nell Cooper

Index